Hey Kids! Let's Visit Seoul South Korea

Fun, Facts, and Amazing Discoveries for Kids

Teresa Mills

Life Experiences Publishing

Contents

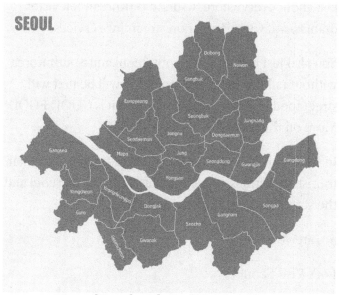

Map of Seoul with Gu (District) Names

Seoul is home to many companies, some that you may have heard of:

- Samsung Electronics

- Hyundai

- Kia

- LG Electronics

South Korea is also very well known for its entertainment industry. K-pop (Korean popular music), with its catchy choruses and rhythms, is popular just about everywhere. K-dramas (Korean television dramas) are very popular on streaming services.

You also just cannot talk about Seoul and South Korea without talking about the food. You will be met with street food vendors everywhere, and it is GOOD FOOD! More on this later.

In this book, we will explore some of the most popular tourist attractions and learn a little history of Seoul and the surrounding area along the way.

So, are you ready?

Let's Visit Seoul!

Welcome

Seoul has a very rich history and is a great place to visit!
Here you will find royal palaces, museums, amazing
shopping districts, a theme park, beautiful urban parks,
and all kinds of food.

This book is written as a fun fact guide about some
attractions and sites in Seoul. It includes some history
interspersed with fun facts about things to do. The
book can easily be enjoyed by younger children through
reading it with them. You can visit Seoul right from your
own home! Whether you are preparing for a vacation
with the family or just want to learn a little more about
Seoul Special City, this book is for you.

As you continue to learn more about Seoul and South
Korea, I have some fun activity and coloring pages that
you can download and print at:

https://kid-friendly-family-vacations.com/seoulfun

When you have completed this book, I invite you to visit the other cities in the series:

Hey Kids! Let's Visit Washington DC
Hey Kids! Let's Visit A Cruise Ship
Hey Kids! Let's Visit New York City
Hey Kids! Let's Visit London England
Hey Kids! Let's Visit San Francisco
Hey Kids! Let's Visit Savannah Georgia
Hey Kids! Let's Visit Paris France
Hey Kids! Let's Visit Charleston South Carolina
Hey Kids! Let's Visit Chicago
Hey Kids! Let's Visit Rome Italy
Hey Kids! Let's Visit Boston
Hey Kids! Let's Visit Philadelphia
Hey Kids! Let's Visit San Diego
Hey Kids! Let's Visit Seattle
Hey Kids! Let's Visit Seoul South Korea

Enjoy!

Teresa Mills

A Little About Seoul

Seoul is located in the northwestern part of the country of South Korea. South Korea is part of the 750-mile-long (1,200 km) Korean Peninsula on the eastern side of the continent of Asia. The map in this chapter might help you understand where Korea is located in Asia.

Seoul's official name is Seoul Special City. Seoul is the capital of South Korea and is its largest metropolitan area. Seoul is a very vibrant, crowded metropolitan city. As a comparison, the population of Seoul is approximately 2 million more than the population of New York City. Seoul is 75 square miles (195 square km) smaller than New York City, though, making it much more crowded. Seoul is a megacity because its population is over 10 million.

Map showing Korea in Eastern Asia

The city of Seoul is divided into 25 different gu, or districts. Gu can be thought of like New York's 5 boroughs (Staten Island, Queens, Brooklyn, Bronx, and Manhattan). Each gu is further separated into dong, or neighborhoods. The map below shows Seoul and its 25 gu. The name of each gu is listed on the map, but when referenced, "gu" is sometimes added to the end. For instance, the gu labeled Jung on the map might be called Jung-gu when being referred to.

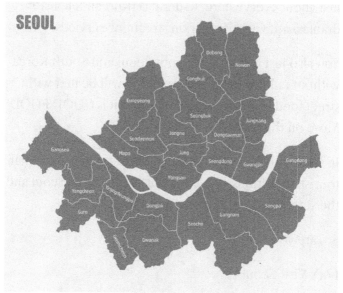

Map of Seoul with Gu (District) Names

Seoul is home to many companies, some that you may have heard of:

- Samsung Electronics

- Hyundai

- Kia

- LG Electronics

South Korea is also very well known for its entertainment industry. K-pop (Korean popular music), with its catchy choruses and rhythms, is popular just about everywhere. K-dramas (Korean television dramas) are very popular on streaming services.

You also just cannot talk about Seoul and South Korea without talking about the food. You will be met with street food vendors everywhere, and it is GOOD FOOD! More on this later.

In this book, we will explore some of the most popular tourist attractions and learn a little history of Seoul and the surrounding area along the way.

So, are you ready?

Let's Visit Seoul!

Chapter 1

The Seoul City Wall

The Fortress Wall around the city of Seoul, also known as the Seoul City Wall, was first built around 1396. It was built to defend the boundaries of the city of Seoul during the Joseon dynasty period. The wall follows the ridges of four mountains around Seoul (Namsan, Naksan, Inwangsan, and Bugaksan) for 11.5 miles (18.5 kilometers).

When the city wall was built, there were four major gates built into the walls. The major gates are at the north, south, east, and west entrances to the city. In between each major gate is a sub-gate. Of the original 8 gates, 6 remain today. About 70% of the original wall, or 8 miles (12.8 kilometers), has been restored or rebuilt.

There are a series of trails around the city today that follow the city wall around Seoul.

The Fortress Wall in Naksan Park

Of the original four main gates, three remain today. Each of the gates has a traditional and a directional name. The remaining main gates are:

Sungnyemun Gate (Namdaemun) – "South Big Gate"

The Namdaemun gate was built between 1396-1398 and for years served as the southern boundary of the city. The Namdaemun gate was heavily damaged by fire in 2008, but it was rebuilt and reopened in 2013. Sungnyemun gate means "Exalted Ceremonies Gate" – it was used by the king to greet and send groups to China.

Sungnyemun (Namdaemun) Gate

Heunginjimun Gate (Dongdaemun) – "East Big Gate"

The Dongdaemun gate is the major eastern gate into the city of Seoul. This gate was the main eastern entrance to the city when originally built. The construction that you see today has been rebuilt from the original and dates back to 1896. Heunginjimun gate means "Rising Benevolence Gate."

Heunginjimun (Dongdaemun) Gate

Sukjeongmun Gate (Bukdaemun) – "North Big Gate"

The Bukdaemun gate is the northernmost gate in the Seoul city wall. The gate was built in 1396 to the north behind Gyeongbokgung Palace. Sukjeongmun gate means "Rule Solemnly Gate."

Sukjeongmun (Bukdaemun) Gate

Fun Facts about the Seoul City Wall

- The section of the city wall that sits along the Sukjeongmun Gate (the northern main gate) was closed for 38 years (1968-2006) due to an assassination attempt on the South Korean president. To visit this area today requires a passport for identification.

- The original wall was built using medium-sized round stones and mud. In the early 1700s, a renovation was started to build the walls with rectangular stone slabs.

- The pathways around the city wall are great hiking paths and are usually very busy with walkers and hikers.

Chapter 2

Korean Royal Palaces

There are five Royal Palaces in Seoul that were built during the Joseon Dynasty. The Joseon Dynasty was the ruling dynasty (a ruling family) of Korea (both North and South were unified) for over 500 years. The Joseon Dynasty ruled from 1392 through the Japanese occupation of Korea in 1910.

These palaces are all located in the center of Seoul and are open for tours. Each of the five major palaces were built during different time periods. But the bottom line is that the palaces are a part of Korea's royal history!

Gyeongbokgung Palace

The Gyeongbokgung Palace was built in 1395 when Seoul became the capital of Korea. Before this time, the capital of Korea was Gaeseong. This palace was the main royal palace of the Joseon dynasty and is the largest and most ornate of all the royal palaces.

Gyeongbokgung Palace

Changdeokgung Palace

This secondary palace is much more in tune with nature than its very ornate sister palace Gyeongbokgung. Most of the palaces were destroyed by the Japanese invasions in the 1500s. This palace was the first one rebuilt after that. Because of that, it served as the main residence of the Joseon dynasty during the 1600-1800s.

Changdeokgung Palace

Changdeokgung Palace has a magical, secret garden called Huwon. It is described as one of the most beautiful places in all of Korea.

Huwon Secret Garden

Deoksugung Palace

Deoksugung Palace was built in 1483 and is a smaller royal palace. This palace is located in the center of the city and does not have a mountain in the background as the others do. This palace was used as the main residence for the dynasty for a while after the 1592 Japanese invasion.

Deoksugung Palace

Changgyeonggung Palace

Changgyeonggung Palace was normally used for visiting nobility to stay while visiting. Also, some of the less important members of the royal family would have lived here. Built in the mid-1400s, it is not as large as some of the other palaces.

The palace was destroyed multiple times during Japanese invasions. Most recently it was destroyed in the early 1900s when it was changed from a palace to a garden. The Japanese then added a botanical garden and a zoo. The zoo was later moved, but the botanical garden is still there.

Changgyeonggung Palace

Gyeonghuigung Palace

Gyeonghuigung Palace is lesser known than the other palaces. It was built in 1617 and was considered a secondary palace. When this palace was in its heyday, it was connected to the Deoksugung Palace by a bridge. It was much larger then, though. Like the other palaces, it was destroyed in the Japanese invasions. The rebuilding of this palace did not start until the 1990s.

Gyeonghuigung Palace

The palace names are long and complicated, but the buildings are amazingly beautiful. Another fun thing that you will see as you stroll around the palace areas are locals and tourists wearing traditional Korean dress called Hanbok. The Hanbok can be rented and worn when touring the palaces. You will see people strolling around wearing the clothes and having their pictures taken.

Woman in Korean Hanbok

Fun Facts about the Korean Royal Palaces

- Geunjeongjeon Hall, located in the Gyeongbokgung Palace, is Korea's largest wooden structure.

- Huwon in Korean means "Secret Garden." The secret garden in Changdeokgung Palace is the largest garden in any of the royal palaces.

- Dancheong is the name of the five colors black, white, yellow, red, and blue. These colors were used to create designs on wooden buildings. These colors can be seen on the palaces around Seoul.

Chapter 3

Korean Foods

South Korea is, in my opinion, a food lover's dream place to visit. While visiting Seoul and South Korea, you owe it to yourself to try as many different dishes as you can. Here are some great choices.

Korean Food

Kimchi

Kimchi is one of the main foods in Korean Cuisine. Kimchi typically is made with fermented and salted vegetables. The most common ingredients are the napa cabbage or Korean radish. The vegetables are seasoned with a big selection of spices and seasonings including ginger, garlic, salted seafood (jeotgal), spring onions, and Korean chili powder (gochugaru). You will find this radish kimchi and other varieties served in just about all restaurants as banchan (Korean side dishes).

Radish Kimchi

Bibimbap

Bibimbap literally means mixed rice. It is one of the most popular of Korean dishes. It is a dish of warm rice with vegetables and spices on top. Then meat (usually beef) and an egg are added to the warm dish. Some cultures in Korea serve a fried egg, while others server it with a raw egg that is then cooked as the food is stirred and eaten.

Bibimbap

Rice Cakes (Tteokbokki)

Korean rice cakes (tteokbokki) are another very popular Korean food. Tteokbokki is a cylindrical rice cake that can be stir-fried with a sauce (either spicy or non-spicy) and served as a dish in on its own. It can also be added to dak galbi or Korean BBQ dishes as well.

Korean Rice Cakes Sauteed in Black Bean Sauce

Bulgogi

Bulgogi is thin sliced pork or beef marinated in a mix of soy sauce, onions, garlic, pepper, and honey. The marinated meat is served with vegetables over rice.

Korean Bulgogi

Kimbap (or Gimbap)

Kimbap is a Korean dish that will remind a lot of people of Japanese sushi. Kimbap is made with white rice stuffed with cooked vegetables and meat and rolled on dried seaweed. There is normally a thin layer of sesame oil on the outside of the seaweed. Koreans enjoy kimbap as a snack or as a meal.

Kimbap

Pajeon (Korean Scallion Pancake)

Pajeon is a savory pancake made with scallions. The term jeon is a term in Korean that is used for dishes coated with wheat flour and egg wash. The word pa means scallion. If the pancake is made with seafood, the term for the pancake is haemul pajeon.

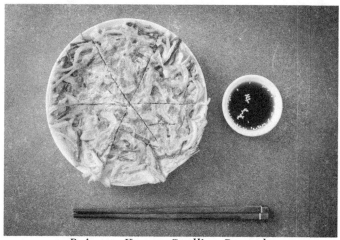

Pajeon - Korean Scallion Pancake

Dak Galbi

The term dak galbi means Korean spicy chicken stir fry. Some restaurants serve the dish with cheese as you see in the picture below.

Dak Galbi with Cheese

Korean BBQ

Korean BBQ is a dish that is really fun to make and eat. The dish consists of a meat – pork belly or beef that is cooked at the table right in front of you is very popular. Once the meat is cooked, it is served in bite size pieces with vegetables and banchan (side dishes) on a piece of crunchy lettuce.

Korean BBQ

Korean Fried Chicken

Korean fried chicken is normally made to have a very thin crackly crust – almost transparent. Before frying, the chicken is seasoned with sugar, salt, and other spices. When frying is complete, the chicken is brushed with a thin layer of sauce.

Korean Fried Chicken

Street Food

Korean street food is everywhere! You will see (and smell) it being cooked in the traditional Korean markets and along the street almost anywhere you go. While there could literally be an entire book written on Korean street food, there are a couple of favorites that I will mention. Also, some of the dishes mentioned above are available as street food such as kimbap, fried chicken, and rice cakes.

Hoetteok are a Korean sweet pancake with a brown sugar filling. Sometimes it also has nuts in the sauce.

Hotteok - Korean Sweet Pancake

Mandu is a meat-filled dumpling that can be served deep fried, pan fried, boiled, or steamed. It is another favorite.

Pork-Filled Mandu

Chapter 4

The War Memorial of Korea

The War Memorial of Korea is a memorial museum that commemorates the 1950-1953 Korean War. Part of the immense history of Korea is the fact that it is currently a divided country. North and South Korea are separated by a heavily militarized border, guarded by a strong army and weapons. North Korea is considered to be the most heavily militarized country in the world.

The purpose of the War Memorial of Korea is:

To contribute to preventing war and achieving peaceful reunification of the country by learning from the lessons of war

The War Memorial of Korea

A Brief History

Korea was once a unified nation (no line between the north and the south) ruled by dynasties and later ruled by Japan. After World War II, Korea was divided between two world powers (the Soviet Union and the United States). After this, from 1945-1948, the Soviet army set up communism in the north, and the United States supported a military (non-communist) government in the south.

In the simplest terms, a communist society is essentially a society that is against democracy (a system of elected officials) and capitalism (an economic system where citizens own businesses, not the government).

In 1948, the United States asked that the United Nations (an intergovernmental organization set up to maintain peace, security, and relationships among nations) to sponsor a vote among all Koreans about the future of the country. The North refused to participate in the vote. The South then formed their own government in Seoul. The North then installed a communist premier in their capital of Pyongyang. The Korean War (1950-1953) was started when North Korea invaded South Korea.

On the grounds of the War Memorial of Korea, there are several statues depicting the hope for peace and reunification as well as the struggles that took place between brothers during the war.

The Statue of Brothers is a two-part statue depicting a South Korean officer and his brother who is North Korean soldier. The lower portion of the statue is a dome with a crack in it. The crack in the statue represents the division between North and South Korea and the hope for its reunification.

Another statue is the 20-foot-high (7-meter) "Shells to Bells" aluminum monument. The bell is formed from shrapnel that was gathered at the DMZ (Demilitarized Zone) between North and South Korea.

Fun Facts about The War Memorial of Korea

- The War Memorial of Korea was built to commemorate victims and veterans of all wars that led to the modern state of South Korea.

- There are many exhibits inside and outside the museum from aircraft and tanks to ships.

- The Brothers Statue (shown in a picture above) is often called the most iconic (representative symbol) of the War Memorial of Korea. It really symbolizes the tragic history of the Korean War.

Chapter 5

National Museum of Korea

This museum was established in 1945 and is committed to research activities in archaeology, art, and history. It was moved to its current location in the Yongsan neighborhood in 2005 and has six galleries set up as permanent exhibits including more than 420,000 artifacts.

The National Museum of Korea is the perfect way to learn about the history and culture of Korea. The museum is very modern and has many high-tech, hands-on exhibits to keep everyone engaged. The museum's exhibits show history through artifacts, paintings, sculptures, and donated collections. The museum even offers a Children's Museum with more hands-on play spaces.

National Museum of Korea

Fun Facts about the National Museum of Korea

- The museum features robots that will help you find specific areas of the museum. Simply let the robot know where you want to go (through a screen), and then follow the robot to the exhibit.

- During the Korean War, the artifacts from this museum were moved south to the city of Busan to avoid destruction.

- Inside the museum is a 44-foot-tall (13.5-meter) stone pagoda from the Gyeongcheonsa Temple site.

Chapter 6

Kimchi Museum (Museum Kimchikan)

The Kimchi Museum is a museum that is dedicated to the history of kimchi. You are able to see everything kimchi including many methods of making this fermented dish and its history. The museum has been in the Insadong neighborhood since 2015 before being located in the Starfield COEX Mall since 1988.

Kimchi is one of the main foods in Korean Cuisine. Kimchi is typically made with fermented and salted vegetables. The most common ingredients are the napa cabbage or Korean radish. The vegetables are seasoned with a big selection of spices and seasonings including ginger, garlic, salted seafood (jeotgal), spring onions, and Korean chili powder (gochugaru).

There are hundreds of different types of kimchi made from different vegetables. The ingredients may depend upon the time of year and what vegetables are available in certain locations. In earlier times, kimchi was stored in large clay fermentation vessels, which could be stored underground in the winter months to prevent freezing. You might also see kimchi vessels stored on special terraces. In more modern times, kimchi refrigerators (special refrigerators to mimic the old underground storage methods) are used for storage.

Kimchi Museum Sign

Banchan is another term that you will hear frequently in Korea. Banchan is a small side dish served with a meal along with rice in a typical Korean meal. Among the banchan is always some kimchi.

Traditional Korean banchan

Fun Facts about the Kimchi Museum

- The Kimchi Museum has a tasting room where you can select and taste some kimchi.

- The museum has a photo zone where you can take pictures of kimchi.

- If you are brave, you can take a look at the Lactobacillus bacteria in kimchi through a microscope.

Chapter 7

N Seoul Tower / Namsan Park

The N Seoul Tower is a local landmark in Seoul. It is 777-feet tall (236.8 meters) so it is easily seen along the Seoul skyline. This height makes it the second highest point in Seoul.

Namsan Park is one of the largest green spaces within the city of Seoul. The park is located in the Myeongdong neighborhood of Seoul. The N Seoul Tower is located at the top of Namsan Mountain.

N Seoul Tower

There are a few ways to get from Namsan Park to the base of the N Seoul Tower.

- The Namsan Cable Car – this option takes about 3 minutes to ride to the tower.

- Bus from the Chungmuro Station or the Dongguk University Station – this can be paid for with a metro card or cash.

- Hiking – there is a main walkway that will take about 30 minutes to get to the top.

Once at the N Seoul Tower, there are many things to do and see. From the lobby area, you will take an elevator to the 5th floor (Tower 5F) observatory. From there, you can then walk to the Tower 4F floor for shops and restaurants as well as views of the city. There are several restaurants taking up entire floors in the tower offering amazing views of the city while you eat.

Fun Facts about the N Seoul Tower

- The N Seoul Tower was the first radio wave tower in the city of Seoul. It was built in 1969 but opened to the public in 1980 as a tourist attraction. The N Seoul tower is still used as a broadcasting tower with up to 48% of the city receiving broadcasts via the tower.

- The N in the name N Seoul Tower stands for New or Namsan. It is also called Seoul Tower and Namsan Tower.

- The tower is illuminated at night in one of four different colors. The colors represent the air quality in and around Seoul. This is used by the city of Seoul to quickly let the public know the air quality. Yellow dust is a problem in Asian countries, so this color indicator lets residents know how the air quality (microdust levels) is. The colors are: Blue – perfect conditions, Green – average air conditions, Yellow – bad conditions, and Red – extremely bad conditions.

Chapter 8

Cheonggyecheon Stream

The Cheonggyecheon Stream is a beautiful public recreation area in downtown Seoul. It's a really nice area to stroll through town.

Cheonggyecheon Stream is the urban restoration project of the stream called Gaecheon that ran through Seoul during the Joseon dynasty. The restoration project began in 2003 and included removing an elevated highway and restoring two historic bridges.

The restored stream opened in 2005. It now runs approximately 6.8 miles (11 kilometers) and passes under 22 bridges.

Cheonggyecheon Stream

Fun Facts about Cheonggyecheon Stream

- The Seoul Lantern Festival is held on the stream every November.

- Late April-mid May, the Lotus Lantern Festival (a UNESCO listed festival) is held celebrating Buddha's birthday. The festival includes a traditional Korean lantern exhibition.

- At Christmas, the stream is decorated to celebrate the holidays.

Chapter 9

Seoul Forest

Seoul Forest is a large park in Seoul. It was opened in 2005 and covers over 3,000 acres (1,200 hectares). In the Seoul Forest, you will find large playgrounds, lots of picnic and resting areas, walking and biking trails, and deer in the ecology forest.

The park is located in the Seongdong-gu district of Seoul which is along the north bank of the Han River. This is a park that residents of Seoul love spending time in – a great place for unwinding and relaxing and just getting away from the hustle and bustle of the big city.

Seoul Forest sign

Every kid, no matter your age, will love playgrounds and climbing. Seoul Forest offers some of the best playgrounds and climbing areas that I have seen anywhere.

One of the many playgrounds is shown here:

Seoul Forest Playground

The slides shown below are built into an existing hill.
What a great idea!

Slides built on a hill on Seoul Forest

Another cool feature is the deer habitat in the Forest. This picture was taken from above the deer habitat on a suspended walkway.

Deer in the Seoul Forest Ecology Park

Fun Facts about the Seoul Forest

- Throughout Seoul Forest you will see over 100 different animals and 400,000 trees.

- Before becoming a public park, the Seoul Forest was used as a royal hunting ground for kings.

- Since 2010, Seoul Forest has created focused programs for youth and teenagers to get outside, look for themselves, and dream outside the classroom.

Chapter 10

Starfield COEX Mall

This is a pretty cool mall to visit in Seoul. The mall is located in the Gangnamgu district of Seoul. Gangnam literally means "south of the river" and that is where it is located – south of the Han River.

The mall is large and has the distinction of being the largest underground mall in the world as of this writing. The mall is 1,650,000 square feet (154,000 square meters) in area. Of that, 1,550,000 square feet (144,000 square meters) are all on one underground floor. The mall boasts of over 100 restaurants that you can try. Other fun things to check out at the mall include:

Starfield Library

One of the most spectacular places in the mall is
the library. In the library, you will find a 43-foot tall
(13-meter) bookshelf in a 30,150 square-foot (2,800
square meter) atrium.

The library has over 70,000 books magazines that are
available for anyone to grab and read while there.

Baskin Robbins 100 Flavor Ice Cream Shop

While the mall has just about anything you can imagine
that a mall would have, they also have a 100-flavor
Baskin Robbins ice cream shop. It's worth a trip to the
mall just to see this ice cream shop!

Starfield Mall Baskin Robbins ice cream selection

COEX Aquarium

The COEX aquarium is one of the largest aquariums in Korea and it is in this mall! The aquarium is set up in an easy-to-follow pathway through 14 different discovery zones (16 if you count the entrance and the gift shop).

Expect to see penguins, sharks, crabs, lionfish and many more that are a part of the more than 40,000 sea animals at the aquarium.

Tropical Fish in the COEX Aquarium

Fun Facts about the Starfield COEX Mall

- The mall has tons of shops, two food courts, an aquarium, and a movie theater.

- The name COEX is a combination of the terms Conference and Exhibition – it is one of the largest conference and exhibition centers in Korea.

- The aquarium in the mall is home to over 600 different marine species.

Chapter 11

Myeongdong Shopping Street

The Myeondong Shopping Street is one place in Seoul to find the best of Korean and international brands. Along the main shopping street, you will find stores such as The Body Shop, Forever 21, Apple, Lacoste, and more. In addition to the brand name stores, you will find restaurants and food stalls.

One of the popular draws to this shopping street is the wide selection of Korean skin care products. You will find brands such as SAEM, Nature Republic, Innisfree, Missha, and Olive Young.

If you are looking for footwear, trendy fashion, skin care, or just about anything else, this is the place to find it.

Myeongdong Shopping Street

In addition to the huge shopping street, the
Myeongdong shopping district includes the Lotte
Department Store flagship store. The bottom floor
(which is huge) is the location of the Lotte Food Avenue.
This is honestly the largest food court that I have ever
seen.

Fun Facts about Myeongdong and the Shopping Street

- Myeongdong is a neighborhood in the Jung district of Seoul. It's a very popular neighborhood for tourists. Myeongdong is a great place to buy K-Pop merch.

- The name Myeongdong Shopping Street is a confusing name as there is not one specific street where the shopping is. It is more of a maze of shopping stores and Korean street food vendors that covers several city blocks.

- Myeongdong Shopping Street is one of the most expensive shopping districts in the world.

Chapter 12

Namdaemun Market

The Namdaemun Market is located in the Myeongdong neighborhood next to Namdaemun, the "south big gate" to the old city (officially named the Sungnyemun Gate). This market is one of the oldest traditional markets still in existence in Korea.

The current Namdaemun Market opened in 1964, but historically it dates back to 1414. It has over 10,000 wholesalers, retailers, and vendors. This is the place to find just about any traditional Korean items including clothing, souvenirs, jewelry, toys, luggage, flowers, electronics, and street food!

The market is alive and active with people at all hours. It is open during the night for retailers to make purchases from the vendors that sell wholesale. Food vendors set up in the evening for the crowds that show up to buy. It is an exciting and vibrant marketplace!

Namdaemun Market

Fun Facts about the Namdaemun Market

- The market covers over 16 acres (6.5 hectares).

- The market was founded during the reign of King Taejong (the third king of the Joseon dynasty).

- The street food scene in Namdaemun Market is some of the best around Seoul. One favorite that you will find cooking daily is the hotteok pancake, a Korean sweet pancake dessert.

Hotteok pancakes at the Namdaemun Market

Chapter 13

Tongin Market Brass Coin Lunchbox

Tongin Market is a traditional Korean street market located in the Tongin-dong neighborhood of the Jongno-gu district of Seoul. The market has been around since 1941 and has about 75 shops and stalls for merchants as well as some restaurants.

The most fun thing about this market was the Yeopjeon Dosirak (Brass Coin Lunchbox), or the Lunchbox Cafe that is part of the market. The Lunchbox Cafe allows visitors to purchase a group of 10 (or multiple groups of 10) brass coins (yeopjeon). These are given with a plastic sectioned plate which you can then take through the market to "taste" different foods.

Food tray and coins at the Tongin Market

Food vendors who participate in the Lunchbox Cafe all display a sign above their food display.

Tongin Market Lunchbox Cafe Participation Sign

Sample size foods can then be purchased from the participating vendor with the brass coins. Food samples normally cost anywhere from 1 to 4 coins.

Food available for brass coins in Tongin Market

Food available for brass coins in Tongin Market

Once you have all the food you would like to try, there are seating areas that provide water and utensils. There is also rice for purchase. It's a great way to sample some Korean street food!

A filled food tray at Tongin Market

Fun Facts about Tongin Market and the Brass Coin Lunchbox

- The Korean word yeopjeon means brass coin. The Korean word dosirak means lunchbox. The cafe is called the Lunchbox Cafe or Dosirak Cafe.

- Tongin Market is not a large traditional market. It is more like a friendly neighborhood market that provides daily needs for the people who live nearby. It's a small neighborhood offering a great food variety for visitors too!

- One of the major attractions in Tongin Market is the Tongin tteokbokki (Korean rice cakes stir-fried in oil). This famous tteokbokki has been around since the start of the Korean War in 1950. The Tongin tteokbokki was featured in a music video for Lee Seung-gi's song, "Invitation to Me."

Chapter 14

Banpo Bridge

The Banpo Bridge connects the Yongsan district and the Seocho district across the Han River. The Banpo bridge is actually the top part of a double decker bridge construction. The bottom bridge you can see in the photo is the Jamsu Bridge. Construction on the bridge was complete in 1982.

The Moonlight Rainbow Fountain is a water show that runs May through October approximately six times a day. The show lasts about 20 minutes. During the water show, the bridge is lighted by more than 200 lights as the fountains shoot out streams of water – all synchronized to music. The jets spray the water out 140 feet (43 meters) and down 65 feet (20 meters) to the Han River.

Banpo Bridge light show

Fun Facts about the Banpo Bridge

- The Banpo Bridge / Jamsu Bridge double deck system was the first double decker bridge in South Korea.

- The lower half of the bridge system (the Jamsu Bridge) is designed to be submerged in water during the rainy season.

- The bridge's fountain is registered in the Guinness Book of World Records as the world's longest bridge fountain.

Chapter 15

Dongdaemun Design Plaza (DDP)

The Dongdaemun Design Plaza (DDP) was designed by architect Zaha Hadid. It is a uniquely designed building that has three stories underground and four stories above ground. It reaches a height of 95 feet (29 meters). The DDP does not have any straight lines or walls.

It is designed as a place where you can Dream, Design, and Play. The DDP is cultural park where you will see conferences, forums, product launches, fashion shows, and exhibitions. The DDP hosts more than 100 exhibitions every year. Product launches such as BMW and Mercedes Benz have taken place at the DDP.

Dongdaumun Design Plaza

The lights, the design, and the events at the DDP give it a very futuristic look. Because of this, it is visited by more than 10 million visitors each year – that's about 30,000 every day.

Fun Facts about the Dongdaemun Design Plaza

The Dongdaemun Design Plaza (DDP) is the largest three-dimensional atypical (not standard looking) building in the world.

Zaha Hadid was the first woman to win the Pritzker Architect Prize (The "Nobel Prize" of Architecture).

The exterior of the building contains 45,133 aluminum panels. None are the same size and pattern.

Chapter 16

Seoul Metro

The Seoul Metro System is one of the cleanest and most well-run mass transit systems that I have seen. The Metro is one of the world's largest urban rail systems. At this time, the rail system has 275 stations and more than 179 miles (289 kilometers) of track. On a given day, there will be more than seven million riders on the trains!

The Seoul Metro system prides itself on being user friendly and providing great customer service. The signs for the stations and the stops along the way are clearly visible and are displayed in multiple languages.

Seoul Metro Station Sign

Seoul Metro Stop Sign

Fun Facts about the Seoul Metro

- Most of the Seoul Metro stations have phone charging stations available for customers.

- The Seoul Metro and its stations are very clean and bright. There are food options and shopping at most locations.

- Despite the system being extremely modern and sparkling clean, it is still one of the least expensive mass transit systems in the world. A basic fare is still just about $1 US.

Chapter 17

KTX Trains

KTX or the Korean Train eXpress is Korea's high speed rail train system. The KTX train system is a high-speed train system that connects the major cities on South Korea. On the high-speed trains, the travel time from Seoul to Busan (the farthest city from Seoul at 204 miles or 329 kilometers) is as little as 2 hours 18 minutes.

These fast trains are called bullet trains. The bullet trains can travel as fast as 189 miles per hour (305 km per hour). A train running its route will have 10 to 20 cars that form the train set.

The train stations are modern and clean, just like the metro stations. Seoul Station is the most popular station and is easily accessible via the Metro system.

Seoul Station

The KTX high speed trains are operated by Korail. The construction process on the train system from Seoul to Busan began in 1992 and service was launched in 2004. While the existing trains and rail system are designed for trains traveling up to 217 miles per hour (350 km per hour), there are trains being tested that will run on conventional rails at 260 miles per hour (420 km per hour).

Fun Facts about the KTX Trains

- In December 2017, a new line was completed to travel to the 2018 Winter Olympics in Pyeongchang, North Korea.

- There has been free WiFi service available on the KTX trains since 2008.

- Travel on the KTX train system is a ticketless and gateless system. When you purchase a ticket for the train, you are assigned a seat. Tickets are purchased on a smart device meaning no paper tickets are printed. The train system staff can then tell which seats are occupied through their phones meaning they do not go seat to seat checking tickets.

Chapter 18

DMZ Tour

The Korean Demilitarized Zone (DMZ) is a zone or a strip of land that basically splits the peninsula of Korea in half, forming North Korea and South Korea. It is really a buffer zone between North and South Korea that was established when the Korean War ended in 1953. At the end of the war, both sides agreed to move their troops back by 1.2 miles (2,000 m / 2 km) creating the 4 km "buffer" zone. This buffer zone is the DMZ (Demilitarized Zone). Splitting the Korean peninsula, the DMZ is 160 miles (257 kilometers) long.

The line down the center of the 4-km buffer zone is called the Military Demarcation Line (MDL). On either side of the MDL is a Limit line – the Northern Limit Line (NLL) and the Southern Limit Line (SLL). The Northern Limit Line is one of the absolute most militarized borders in the entire world. The DMZ area is where all negotiations are held when talks of reunification take place. The DML is marked by signposts placed 6 feet (2 meters) apart.

From Seoul, there is a tour that will take visitors to the DMZ. It is a very interesting tour and a very real part of the history of Korea.

The tour consists of visiting three locations:

- The Imjingak Peace Park – a place where North Korean refugees were welcomed and consoled during the Korean War.

- The 3rd Tunnel – an infiltration tunnel discovered in 1978. This is a tunnel that was dug by the North Koreans to try to infiltrate into South Korea. Here you have the opportunity to walk 540 ft (165 m) into the tunnel to the first of three blockades built to prevent further moving through the tunnel. At this point, you are 560 ft (170 m) from the MDL.

- The Dora Observatory – an observatory on top of a hill close to the 3rd tunnel where you can view villages in North Korea.

Visiting and being able to cross into the Demilitarized Zone is a unique experience, and not one to take lightly. It is very sobering to realize that there is still such a zone as this today.

I hope you enjoyed your trip to Seoul! I have a fun puzzle and coloring pages to go along with the book. These are free to download here:

kid-friendly-family-vacations.com/seoulfun

———————————————————————————

If you enjoyed your visit to Seoul, please leave a review to help others also learn more about Seoul whether traveling or learning from home.

kid-friendly-family-vacations.com/review-seoul

———————————————————————————

Next, let's head to Europe to visit Rome Italy where we will learn what it's like to have one of the seven wonders of the world right downtown!

kid-friendly-family-vacations.com/booktour-rome

———————————————————————————

Want to visit the US West Coast? Let's visit Seattle where you will find a 605 feet (184 meters) needle in downtown!

kid-friendly-family-vacations.com/booktour-seattle

———————————————————————————

Visit all the cities in the Hey Kids! Let's Visit series...

kid-friendly-family-vacations.com/series

Also By Teresa Mills and Kid Friendly Family Vacations

Hey Kids! Let's Visit Washington DC
Hey Kids! Let's Visit A Cruise Ship
Hey Kids! Let's Visit New York City
Hey Kids! Let's Visit London England
Hey Kids! Let's Visit San Francisco
Hey Kids! Let's Visit Savannah Georgia
Hey Kids! Let's Visit Paris France
Hey Kids! Let's Visit Charleston South Carolina
Hey Kids! Let's Visit Chicago
Hey Kids! Let's Visit Rome Italy
Hey Kids! Let's Visit Boston
Hey Kids! Let's Visit Philadelphia
Hey Kids! Let's Visit San Diego
Hey Kids! Let's Visit Seattle
Hey Kids! Let's Visit Seoul South Korea

More from Kid Friendly Family Vacations

BOOKS

Books to help build your kids / grandkids life
experiences through travel and learning
https://kid-friendly-family-vacations.com/books

COLORING AND ACTIVITY PAGKAGES

Coloring pages, activity books, printable travel journals,
and more in our Etsy shop
https://kid-friendly-family-vacations.com/etsy

RESOURCES FOR TEACHERS

Resources for teachers on Teachers Pay Teachers
https://kid-friendly-family-vacations.com/tpt

It is our mission to help you build your children's
and grand-children's life experiences through travel.
Not just traveling with your kids... building their Life
Experiences"! Join our community here:
https://kid-friendly-family-vacations.com/join

Heunginjimun gate- © sepavone / depositphotos.com

Sukjeongmun gate- © thomaslenne / depositphotos.com

Korean Food – variety - © VadimVasenin / depositphotos.com

Korean food - kimbap - © bhofack2 / depositphotos.com

Koran food – radish kimchi - © asimojet / depositphotos.com

Korean food - bibimbap - © alex9500 / depositphotos.com

Korean food – rice cakes - © topntp / depositphotos.com

Korean food - bulgogi - © stockphoto81 / depositphotos.com

Korean food - pajeon - © topntp / depositphotos.com

Korean food - dak galbi - © Kid Friendly Family Vacations

Korean food - Korean bbq - © romixcontact@gmail.com / depositphotos.com

Korean food - Korean fried chicken - © topntp / depositphotos.com

Korean food - hotteok - © Anneylier /
depositphotos.com

Korean food - mandu - © bhofack2 /
depositphotos.com

Gyeongbokgung Palace - © sepavone /
depositphotos.com

Changdeokgung Palace - © SangaPark /
depositphotos.com

Changdeokgung Secret Garden - Huwon - ©
OlezzoSimona / depositphotos.com

Deoksugung Palace - © aaron90311 /
depositphotos.com

Changgyeonggung Palace - © photo_jeong /
depositphotos.com

Gyeonghuigung Palace - © siavramova /
depositphotos.com

Korean Hanbok - ©
praewa_koreashopping@hotmail.com /
depositphotos.com

The War Memorial of Korea - sign - © Kid Friendly
Family Vacations

National Museum of Korea - main building - © Kid
Friendly Family Vacations

Kimchi Museum - © Kid Friendly Family Vacations

Banchan - © Kid Friendly Family Vacations

N Seoul Tower / Namsan Park
- © praewa_koreashopping@hotmail.com /
depositphotos.com

Cheonggyecheon Stream - © TKKurikawa /
depositphotos.com

Seoul Forest - sign - © Kid Friendly Family Vacations

Seoul Forest - playground - © Kid Friendly Family
Vacations

Seoul Forest - slides - © Kid Friendly Family Vacations

Seoul Forest - deer - © Kid Friendly Family Vacations

Starfield - ice cream - © Kid Friendly Family Vacations

Starfield – tropical fish at aquarium - © iggy74 /
depositphotos.com

Myeongdong Shopping Street - © Kid Friendly Family
Vacations

Namdaemun Market - © jannystockphoto /
depositphotos.com

Namdaemun - hotteok pancake -
© praewa_koreashopping@hotmail.com /
depositphotos.com

Tongin Market - tray - © Kid Friendly Family Vacations

Tongin Market - participation sign - © Kid Friendly Family Vacations

Tongin Market – food selection 1 - © Kid Friendly Family Vacations

Tongin Market – food selection 2 - © Kid Friendly Family Vacations

Tongin Market – full tray - © Kid Friendly Family Vacations

Banpo Bridge - © nattanai / depositphotos.com

Dongdaemun Design Plaza (DDP) - © Kathryn Welch

Seoul Metro - © Kid Friendly Family Vacations

Seoul Station - © Kid Friendly Family Vacations

About the Author

Teresa Mills is the bestselling author of the "Hey Kids! Let's Visit..." Book Series for Kids! Teresa's goal through her books and website is to help parents / grandparents who want to build the life experiences of their children / grandchildren through travel and learning activities.

She is an active mother and Mimi. She and her family love traveling in the USA, and internationally too! They love exploring new places, eating cool foods, and having yet another adventure as a family! With the Mills, it's all about traveling as family.

In addition to traveling, Teresa enjoys reading, hiking, biking, and helping others.

Join in the fun at

kid-friendly-family-vacations.com